GENERATION AI

The Next Generation Born into an AI World

RENE MULBERY

Copyright © 2023 RENE MULBURY

All rights reserved

The characters and events portrayed in this book are fictitious. Any similarity to real persons, living or dead, is coincidental and not intended by the author.

No part of this book may be reproduced, or stored in a retrieval system, or transmitted in any form or by any means, electronic, mechanical, photocopying, recording, or otherwise, without express written permission of the publisher.

ISBN: 9798376454763

Cover design by: RENE MULBURY
Library of Congress Control Number: 2018675309
Printed in the United States of America

CONTENTS

Title Page
Copyright
Dedication
Introduction
Growing Up in an AI World   1
Education and Skills for the AI Era   12
The Ethics and Social Implications of AI   23
Exploring the Potential of AI for Good   33
Conclusion   42
Acknowledgments   51

DEDICATION

To all the parents, teachers, mentors, and leaders who are working tirelessly to guide our next generation into a world dominated by artificial intelligence.

You are the ones who will shape the future by providing the children of today with the tools, values, and perspectives they need to thrive in a rapidly changing world. Your dedication to their well-being, growth, and success is truly inspiring, and it is through your efforts that the next generation will be equipped to make the most of the opportunities and challenges that lie ahead.

We cannot predict the exact shape that the future will take, but we can be confident that it will be shaped in large part by the children of today. They are the ones who will grow up with AI as a ubiquitous presence in their lives, and they will be the ones who will shape the way that AI is used and developed.

This book is dedicated to all of you who are working to prepare the next generation for this exciting, uncertain, and critical future. Your tireless efforts will ensure that our children will have the skills, knowledge, and values they need to make the world a better place for all. May your work be blessed and may the future be bright for all the children of the AI era.

INTRODUCTION

The world as we know it is changing, and at the forefront of this change is Artificial Intelligence. AI is everywhere, infiltrating our lives in ways we never could have imagined just a few short years ago. It is in our homes, our workplaces, and even our pockets, shaping the way we think, feel, and interact with the world. But what exactly is AI, and what impact is it having on our society?

Artificial Intelligence, at its most basic definition, refers to the development of computer systems that can perform tasks that would typically require human intelligence, such as learning, problem-solving, and decision-making. It is a field that has been around for decades, but only in recent years has it become a ubiquitous presence in our lives, powering everything from Siri and Alexa to self-driving cars and medical diagnoses.

As AI has become more widespread, its impact on society has grown along with it. On one hand, AI has the potential to revolutionize the way we live and work, improving our efficiency and freeing us from repetitive, menial tasks. It has the power to improve our health, protect our environment, and even extend our lives. But AI also poses significant challenges and risks to society, from job loss and economic inequality to ethical dilemmas and privacy concerns.

It is impossible to ignore the impact that AI is having on our world. It is changing the way we interact with technology, and it is changing the way we think about the future. As we move deeper into the AI era, we must be mindful of both its potential and its pitfalls, and work to shape its development in a way that helps all of us.

But for now, the future stays uncertain. Will AI be the answer to our problems, or will it bring about new challenges that we never could have predicted? Only time will tell, but one thing is clear: the impact of AI on our society will be one of the defining stories of our time.

Kids born under AI control

They are the first generation to grow up surrounded by AI, to have robots and algorithms as a part of their everyday lives. They are the kids born under AI control, and they are unlike any generation that has come before them.

For these kids, technology is not foreign or intimidating. It is not something they have to learn or adapt to. It is simply a part of whom they are, woven into the fabric of their lives from the very beginning. They are the first true digital natives, born into a world where AI is not a novelty, but a necessity.

But what does it mean to grow up surrounded by AI? What impact will it have on these kids, both in the short term and in the long term? These are questions that are just beginning to be explored, but early indications are that the impact will be profound.

For one thing, these kids will be more tech-savvy and technologically literate than any earlier generation. They will have a natural understanding of how technology works, and they will be able to use it in ways that we can only imagine. But beyond that, they will also have a unique perspective on the world, shaped by their experiences growing up with AI.

Will they view AI as a tool to be used, or as a partner to be respected? Will they see robots as friends or as foes? Will they be comfortable relying on algorithms to make decisions for them, or will they push back against the idea of AI control? These are all questions that will be answered in time, but for now, the concept of kids born under AI control still is a mystery.

One thing is clear, however: the world will never be the same once these kids come of age. They will bring with them a new way of thinking about technology, and a new way of engaging with the world. And for better or for worse, they will be shaping our future in ways that we can only begin to imagine.

Questions we will explore

The world is rapidly evolving with technology advancing at an unprecedented pace, and AI is becoming increasingly integrated into our daily lives. This book investigates the impact of AI on society and raises important questions about its future.

We will delve into the implications of kids growing up in an AI-dominated world and the impact on their lives and the lives of those around them. It examines the role of technology in our lives and the meaning of being human in an increasingly technological world.

This book encourages critical thinking about the future of AI and its impact on society, including the ethical and moral implications of creating truly intelligent machines. It explores the changes AI is bringing to our work, economy, and interactions with one another and considers the future of work in an AI-driven world.

I will challenge readers to confront their assumptions about technology and consider what it means to be human in an AI-driven world. It serves as a call to action, reminding us that the future is shaped by our choices and actions and that we have a responsibility to make informed decisions about AI's role in our lives and the lives of future generations.

GROWING UP IN AN AI WORLD

How AI will shape kids development

The impact of AI on childhood development is multifaceted and complex. On one hand, AI has the potential to enhance children's learning and provide them with access to a wealth of information and resources. For example, AI-powered educational tools can help children learn new skills and information at their own pace, supplying individualized and personalized instruction that is tailored to their needs.

However, on the other hand, the constant presence of AI in children's lives can also have negative effects on their development. Children are spending increasing amounts of time interacting with screens and digital devices, and this can have a significant impact on their mental and emotional well-being. Studies have shown that excessive screen time is associated with increased levels of anxiety, depression, and attention deficit hyperactivity disorder (ADHD) in children.

One of the main concerns about AI's impact on childhood development is its effect on children's relationships and social skills. Children are growing up in a world where many of their social interactions are mediated through screens and digital devices, rather than face-to-face interactions. This can lead to difficulties in forming meaningful connections with others and can hurt their ability to develop healthy relationships and social skills.

In addition, the impact of AI on childhood development can also extend to children's sense of self and identity. Someone constantly bombarded children with images and messages from the media, and these images and messages can shape their views of themselves and the world around them. AI algorithms that personalize content based on individual preferences can worsen these effects, leading to a distorted view of reality and an over-reliance on technology to confirm their sense of self.

It is important to consider the psychological impact of AI on childhood development and to develop strategies to mitigate its negative effects. This can include promoting healthy screen time habits, encouraging children to engage in activities that promote social and emotional development, and teaching children critical thinking skills so that they can better understand and navigate the digital world.

While AI has the potential to enhance childhood development in various ways, it is important to be mindful of its potential to cause harm. As we continue to study the impact of AI on childhood development, we must work to balance its benefits with the need to protect the health and well-being of the next generation.

The impact of AI on the daily lives of children

As a parent, I have seen firsthand the impact that technology has on the daily lives of kids. The rise of AI has brought with it a new era of convenience and accessibility, but it has also created unique challenges and concerns.

For kids growing up in an AI-driven world, technology is a ubiquitous part of their daily experience. From an early age, screens and digital devices surround them, using them to communicate, learn, play, and socialize. AI-powered virtual assistants, smart home devices, and other technologies have become fixtures in their lives, offering new ways to interact with the world around them.

However, this heavy dependence on technology and AI also raises questions about its impact on kids' development. Research suggests that excessive screen time can interfere with children's ability to regulate their emotions and behavior and may negatively affect their attention span and sleep patterns. Kids' exposure to online content, such as social media, can lead to feelings of anxiety, depression, and decreased self-esteem.

We must examine the role that technology and AI play in kids' lives and consider the steps we can take to promote healthy and balanced usage. This includes setting the right limits on screen time, promoting healthy digital habits, and encouraging kids to engage in activities that foster their emotional, social, and cognitive development.

Technology and AI are here to stay and will continue to shape the lives of kids in the coming years. As a society, it is our responsibility to ensure that we are using these tools in ways that promote their growth and well-being.

The impact of AI on family dynamics and relationships

I have seen firsthand how technology has transformed family dynamics and relationships. The increasing prevalence of AI-powered devices and services has brought new challenges and opportunities to families, changing how they communicate, interact, and spend time together.

One of the most notable changes is how technology and AI have affected the way families communicate. With smartphones, laptops, and other devices constantly at our fingertips, we are more connected than ever before, but this constant connectivity can also create alternative sources of conflict and tension. Family members may feel ignored or disrespected when others are on their devices during mealtimes or other important moments, leading to feelings of isolation and disconnection.

AI-powered devices and services have disrupted traditional family routines and activities. For example, smart home devices and virtual assistants have made household tasks such as cooking, cleaning, and grocery shopping easier and more efficient, but they have also altered the way families spend time together. Instead of cooking meals together or completing household chores together, family members may now use AI to complete these tasks more quickly, reducing the time they spend interacting with one another.

Another challenge posed by AI is the impact it may have on children's development and behavior. As children spend more time interacting with screens and digital devices, they may have fewer opportunities to develop social and emotional skills and may struggle to understand and manage their emotions in real-world situations. They may also become more reliant on AI for information and guidance, leading to decreased independence and critical thinking skills.

Despite these challenges, AI has also brought new opportunities for families to connect and bond. For example, social media and other online platforms have supplied new avenues for families to stay in touch, even when they are physically separated. AI-powered devices and services have made it easier for families to manage their busy schedules and complete household tasks, freeing up more time for shared experiences and activities.

The impact of AI on family dynamics and

relationships is complex and multifaceted. While it has brought new challenges and concerns, it has also created new opportunities for connection and growth. As a society, we must continue to examine how AI is affecting families and work together to ensure that it is being used in ways that promote healthy relationships and well-being.

The challenges and opportunities

One of the biggest challenges for kids born under AI control is navigating the complex relationship between humans and machines. These kids are growing up in a world where AI is integrated into every aspect of their lives, from the devices they used to communicate with friends and family, to the systems that regulate the temperature in their homes. While this integration supplies many benefits, such as increased efficiency and convenience, it also raises questions about what it means to be human in an age dominated by technology.

Another challenge for kids born under AI control is developing their sense of self and independence. With AI supplying answers and solutions at their fingertips, there is a risk of these kids becoming too dependent on technology and lacking the critical thinking and critical thinking skills that are essential for success in the modern world.

Despite these challenges, there are also many opportunities for kids born under AI control. For example, AI can provide these kids with access to vast amounts of information and resources that would have been difficult or impossible to obtain just a few decades ago. AI can also help these kids stay connected with friends and family, even when they are physically apart, fostering a sense of community and belonging.

Kids born under AI control face unique challenges and opportunities, shaped by the constant presence of technology in their lives. As a parent, I hope that we can help these kids navigate this complex landscape, developing their sense of self, independence, and critical thinking skills, while also taking advantage of the many benefits that AI can provide.

EDUCATION AND SKILLS FOR THE AI ERA

The role of AI in education and learning

I have had the privilege of watching the integration of AI in the classroom evolve over the years. At first, I was skeptical about its impact on learning and teaching. However, I have come to realize the potential AI has in revolutionizing the way we approach education and learning.

One of the most significant benefits of AI in education is its ability to personalize learning. With AI algorithms, students can receive tailored learning experiences that are based on their individual needs, strengths, and weaknesses. This is particularly crucial in a classroom setting where students have diverse learning styles and abilities.

Another advantage of AI in education is the ability to supply instant feedback to students. For example, AI-powered writing tools can supply suggestions on grammar, spelling, and punctuation, allowing students to receive immediate feedback and make corrections in real-time. This improves the writing process, making it more efficient and effective.

AI can also provide teachers with valuable data

and insights about their students. With AI tools, teachers can watch students' progress, name areas where they may be struggling, and supply more support to help them succeed.

However, it is essential to recognize that AI is not a silver bullet for all education problems. While AI can supply a wealth of benefits, it is essential to keep in mind that technology should never replace human interaction and critical thinking. A teacher's role is to help learning and supply guidance, and that cannot be replaced by technology.

AI is a tool that can revolutionize the way we approach education and learning. By personalizing learning experiences, supplying instant feedback, and supplying valuable insights, AI has the potential to create a more efficient and effective learning environment. However, it is essential to remember that technology is only a tool, and it is up to teachers to decide the best way to use it to meet the needs of their students.

*Preparing kids for a future
workforce dominated by AI*

I am constantly thinking about how I can prepare my students for a transforming world. Today, it has become increasingly clear that Artificial Intelligence (AI) is going to play a significant role in shaping our future workforce. We must equip our kids with the skills and knowledge they will need to thrive in a world where AI is prevalent.

The Importance of Adaptability:

One of the most critical skills that kids will need in a future dominated by AI is the ability to adapt. AI is advancing at an unprecedented rate, and recent technologies are appearing all the time. As a result, the job market is constantly developing, and we must equip kids with the skills necessary to pivot and adapt to new situations.

Emphasizing Critical Thinking and Problem-Solving:

Another critical skill that kids will need in a future workforce dominated by AI is the ability to think critically and solve problems. AI is a tool that can automate routine tasks and make processes more efficient. However, it is important to remember that AI cannot replace the human mind's ability to think creatively and solve complex problems.

The Importance of Human Connection:

As AI continues to advance, kids must understand the importance of human connection. While AI can help us automate sufficient tasks, it can never replace the human touch. Kids will need to understand how to work effectively with others, communicate effectively, and build meaningful relationships.

Example:

To illustrate the importance of these skills, I would like to share a case study from a classroom. A student, Sarah, was always a strong student academically. However, she struggled with adapting to recent technologies and working effectively with others. Over time, I noticed that Sarah's peers were bypassing her in class discussions and group projects, even though she had a solid understanding of the material.

To help Sarah develop these essential skills, The teacher started incorporating more collaborative projects into the lessons and encouraged her to take part in class discussions. She helped her develop a growth mindset and taught her how to be more adaptable and open-minded when faced with innovative technologies.

In a matter of months, Sarah's confidence grew, and she became a more active participant. She also excelled in her group projects, using her critical thinking and critical thinking skills to produce creative solutions to complex problems.

Conclusion:

It has been exciting to see the impact that a focus on adaptability, critical thinking, and human connection can have on a student's success. I believe that by prioritizing these skills, we can help prepare kids for a future workforce dominated by AI. By teaching kids to be adaptable, critical thinkers, and effective communicators, we can help them thrive in a rapidly changing world.

The skills and qualities that will be essential in the AI era

It is important to consider the changing landscape of the workforce and prepare our students for the challenges and opportunities of the future. One of the biggest shifts that we are currently seeing is the increasing dominance of Artificial Intelligence (AI) in various industries. The world of work is exploding, and we must equip the next generation with the skills and qualities they will need to thrive in this unfamiliar environment.

One of the most significant changes brought on by the rise of AI is the nature of work itself. Automation and machine learning algorithms are replacing many traditional jobs, while new roles appear that require a distinct set of skills. As a result, we must teach our students to be flexible in their approach to learning and work. They must be able to develop new skills and technologies and be comfortable with change.

Another critical skill in the AI era is creativity. Machines may perform tasks faster and more efficiently than humans, but they cannot think creatively and produce novel solutions to problems. We must encourage our students to develop their creative thinking skills, so they can find innovative ways to apply technology to real-world problems.

Collaboration and teamwork are also increasingly important in the AI era. As machines take over more routine tasks, it will be necessary for people to work together to create innovative solutions and find new ways to use technology. Our students must learn to work well in teams and understand the value of collaboration.

Finally, we must teach our students to have a strong ethical and moral compass. As machines become more advanced and autonomous, we must ensure we programmed them to act in ways that are responsible, fair, and just. We must equip our students with a strong moral foundation and be able to make ethical decisions in a transforming world.

The skills and qualities needed to thrive in the AI era differ from those that were necessary for the past. As teachers and educators, it is our responsibility to help our students develop the skills they need to succeed in this rapidly changing world. By fostering creativity, collaboration, adaptability, and a strong moral foundation, we can help ensure that the next generation is ready for the challenges and opportunities of the AI era.

The challenges and opportunities presented by AI in education

As our world continues to grow and adapt to integrating technology, I constantly ponder the impact this has on various aspects of our lives, including education. This chapter will delve into how Artificial Intelligence (AI) is transforming the field of education and the skills and qualities that students must have to thrive in this changing landscape.

AI supplies an exciting opportunity to revolutionize the way we approach learning by enabling personalized instruction. Using student data, AI can assess patterns and preferences to deliver customized content and resources, leading to more efficient and effective learning experiences.

However, some challenges accompany this integration, one of which is the potential for a decrease in creativity and critical thinking skills. When students become too reliant on AI to complete tasks and solve problems, they may struggle to develop the ability to think freely and generate innovative ideas.

Educators must prepare students for a future workforce that AI. will probably dominate.

To achieve this, they must focus on cultivating skills such as problem-solving, critical thinking, and communication, as well as qualities such as empathy, creativity, and adaptability. Technology can not replicate these skills and qualities, and they will be in high demand in the AI era.

Integrating AI into education presents both opportunities and challenges, and it's up to educators to ensure students are well-equipped for success in this new era. This requires a commitment to personalized learning, critical thinking, problem-solving, and creativity, and a focus on preparing students for a future dominated by AI.

THE ETHICS AND SOCIAL IMPLICATIONS OF AI

The impact of AI on personal privacy and autonomy

I have seen first-hand the impact that technology has had on people's lives. From the way we communicate to the way we work, the influence of AI has been immense. But one area that is particularly concerning is the impact of AI on personal privacy and autonomy.

The development of AI has brought with it numerous benefits, but it has also raised questions about what it means to be human. As AI systems become more sophisticated, it is becoming increasingly difficult to understand who or what is deciding and how those decisions are being made. This has led to concerns about the loss of privacy, as increased data is collected and analyzed, and the potential for AI systems to make decisions that are harmful to individuals.

In a world where AI systems are increasingly becoming a part of our daily lives, we must consider the impact they have on our privacy and autonomy. It is not just a question of how we can use AI systems to make our lives easier or more convenient, but a question of what kind of society we want to create.

We must consider the moral implications of AI and its impact on privacy and autonomy. We must strive to create an AI-powered future that is fair, just, and respectful of individual rights and freedoms. Only by doing so can we ensure that all that share the benefits of AI support our humanity in a world dominated by technology.

*The responsibility of society
to shape the development of
AI in ethical and fairways*

I am acutely aware of the potential of AI to shape the world. Its impact on society will be vast and far-reaching, and it is our responsibility as a community to ensure that this development occurs ethically and equitably.

The rise of AI presents sufficient opportunities, including improved efficiency, better decision-making, and breakthroughs in scientific research. However, it also presents various challenges, including the potential for widespread job loss, the risk of worsening existing inequalities, and the threat to personal privacy and autonomy.

We must take an initiative-taking approach to shape the development of AI in a way that helps all members of society. This requires that we ponder the ethical implications of each recent development and ensure that I heard the voices of marginalized communities. It also requires that we invest in research and development that is focused on creating AI systems that are transparent, accountable, and designed to support the greater good.

We also ensure that the benefits of AI are distributed equitably so that everyone has access to the opportunities it presents. This means investing in education and training programs that will help people adapt to the changing workforce and creating policies that support those who are most vulnerable to the effects of technological change.

I am committed to working towards these goals, and to fostering a society that is responsible, ethical, and fair in its approach to AI. This is not just a matter of technological progress, but a matter of fundamental human values and the common good. It is a challenge that we must all accept, together, to build a future that is bright and hopeful for generations to come.

RENE MULBERY

The importance of teaching kids about the ethical implications of AI

It is our responsibility to equip the next generation with the knowledge and understanding to navigate the ethical implications of AI. The advancements in AI have the potential to help society, but it is crucial that we also consider the impact it may have on privacy, autonomy, and personal values.

We ensure that the use of AI aligns with the principles of fairness, equality, and respect for individual rights. To achieve this, we must educate the young minds of today about the potential consequences of AI and how they can use it for the greater good.

Teaching kids about the ethical implications of AI means instilling in them a sense of moral responsibility. They must understand the importance of respecting privacy, avoiding discriminatory practices, and ensuring that AI is used for the benefit of all, not just a privileged few.

They need to be informed of the potential dangers that come with AI, such as losing privacy, the spread of misinformation, and the potential for the manipulation of public opinion. With this knowledge, they can be the guardians of their privacy and autonomy and help shape the development of AI in ethical and fairways.

The education of the next generation about the ethical implications of AI is essential to ensure that it is developed and used in a way that is beneficial to all. It is our duty as leaders to prepare them for this task so that they can become informed, responsible, and ethical leaders of tomorrow.

The need for kids to understand and contribute to the debate about the future of AI

As we stand on the cusp of an AI-driven world, we must consider the impact this technology will have on our lives and our future. And no one is more important in this discussion than the next generation of kids born into this world. They are the ones who will inherit the consequences of the decisions we make now and must be equipped to engage in the ongoing discourse about the role and direction of AI.

At its core, the development of AI raises complex and profound questions about the very nature of humanity. How do we balance the benefits of AI with the potential risks it poses? What does it mean to be human in a world increasingly dominated by machines? How do we ensure that AI serves the interests of all people, not just a privileged few?

As a thinker, it is the responsibility of society to engage in these debates and to ensure that the next generation is equipped to contribute meaningfully. This means providing kids with a deep understanding of the technology, its implications, and the ethical considerations involved. It means helping them develop the critical thinking and critical thinking skills they need to engage in these debates and make informed decisions about their own lives and the world they will inherit.

In short, the future of AI is not something that can be left to chance. It is something we must actively shape, and that requires the active engagement of all members of society, including our kids. By providing them with the knowledge, skills, and tools they need to understand and contribute to these debates, we can help ensure that the future of AI serves the interests of all people, promotes the common good, and upholds the values we hold dear.

EXPLORING THE POTENTIAL OF AI FOR GOOD

*The role of AI in solving global
problems and creating a better future*

I believe that the role of AI in solving global problems and creating a better future is a complex and multifaceted issue. On the one hand, AI has the potential to provide us with innovative solutions to some of the world's most pressing challenges, such as climate change, poverty, and disease. For example, AI algorithms can analyze vast amounts of data to show patterns and predict future trends, which can help us better understand and address these issues.

AI also presents some significant ethical and moral dilemmas. For example, the development of AI systems that can make decisions that change people's lives raises questions about accountability and responsibility. Who will be responsible if an AI system causes harm or makes a mistake? How can we ensure we designed AI systems in a way that protects human dignity and rights?

I believe that the role of AI in solving global problems and creating a better future depends on how society uses it. We must strive to use AI in ways that are ethical, fair, and aligned with our values and priorities. This requires ongoing dialogue and debate about the future of AI, as well as investments in education and research that can help us to understand and shape its development.

We must educate future generations about the potential benefits and challenges of AI. By encouraging kids to understand and contribute to the debate about the future of AI, we can help to ensure that it develops in ways that are consistent with our values and that help all of humanity.

The potential for kids to shape the development of AI for the common good

The future of AI and the impact it will have on our world heavily depend on the next generation. Children are the architects of tomorrow, and it is through their education, thoughts, and actions that the future of AI will be determined. Hence, they must be equipped with the skills and knowledge to critically evaluate and shape the role of AI in their lives and the world.

An essential aspect of their education should be to understand the ethical and moral implications of AI and its impact on society, including the social, economic, and political implications. But merely preparing them for a future with AI is not enough. We must empower them to be proactive agents in the shaping of this future by fostering their creativity, inquisitiveness, and sense of responsibility.

It is crucial to instill in them a vision for using AI to solve global problems, such as climate change, poverty, and disease. By encouraging them to think of AI as a tool for positive change, they will develop a more comprehensive understanding of its potential.

In conclusion, the next generation has a tremendous role to play in deciding the future of AI. It is up to us as educators, leaders, and society to support and guide them in this quest, ensuring that the future of AI is for the greater good of all people and the planet.

For example, imagine a student who is passionate about solving the problem of climate change. With the help of AI, they can analyze and interpret data to develop innovative solutions to mitigate its impact. This could range from designing smart energy systems that reduce carbon emissions to creating algorithms that predict and mitigate the effects of natural disasters. Through education, empowerment, and inspiration, we can help the next generation shape a future where AI is used for the benefit of all.

The importance of fostering creativity and innovation

It is often seen that technology and humanity intersect, leading to significant impacts on shaping our world. The emergence of artificial intelligence is no exception. The rapid advancement in AI technology poses significant implications, especially for the younger generation. In this chapter, I want to delve into the significance of promoting creativity and innovation in the age of AI.

Creativity and innovation have always been central to human advancement. They fuel new ideas, spark new ways of thinking, and lead to breakthroughs in fields such as science, art, and technology. As AI becomes increasingly intertwined with our daily lives, it is crucial to nurture and stimulate creativity and innovation in our children.

While AI technology has the potential to automate various tasks, it also presents new opportunities for creative thinking. By fostering creativity and innovation, we are providing children with the skills they need to succeed in a world dominated by AI.

Fostering creativity and innovation in the age of AI is not only about preparing children for their future careers. It is also about empowering them to influence the future of AI itself. Children equipped with creative thinking skills will have the ability to contribute to the development of AI in ways that benefit society.

The rise of AI presents both challenges and opportunities for the upcoming generation. By promoting creativity and innovation in our children, we can encourage them to become active participants in shaping the future of AI and ensure that its development serves the greater good. For example, a child who has a passion for environmental sustainability could use their creativity and innovation skills to develop AI solutions to tackle global warming.

The role of kids in creating a fairer and more sustainable world with the help of AI

As we navigate the intersection of technology and humanity, it's fascinating to consider the impact that AI will have on our future. The rapid advancements in AI raise important questions about what role kids born in the AI era will play in shaping our world.

Picture this: kids using AI to create new and innovative solutions to some of the world's most pressing problems, like poverty, inequality, and environmental degradation. Imagine kids taking an active role in shaping the future of AI to be more inclusive, fair, and sustainable, guided by their unique perspectives and ideas.

To make this a reality, we must empower kids to become creative thinkers and analytical people. By fostering their critical thinking skills and encouraging their curiosity, we can help them develop a love for innovation and creativity, skills that are uniquely human and essential in the AI era.

But it's not just about preparing them for future careers. It's also about helping them understand the ethical implications of AI and taking an active role in shaping its development. By learning about the challenges facing our planet, kids can develop a sense of global responsibility and use their creative thinking skills to help solve the world's problems.

Take, for example, a group of kids who are passionate about sustainability. With the help of AI, they could design new technologies that are more energy-efficient and environmentally friendly. Or, they could advocate for policies that prioritize the well-being of people and the planet. The possibilities are endless, and it's all within reach for kids born in the AI era.

The role of kids in shaping the future of AI is exciting and full of potential. By supporting and encouraging them to be active participants, we can help ensure that the future of AI is shaped by human values and aspirations and that it works for everyone. Let's empower the next generation to shape their future and the future of AI!

CONCLUSION

I have spent time contemplating the themes and questions explored in this book. The notion of a new generation born under AI control is both exciting and daunting. It stands for a seismic shift in our understanding of what it means to be human and the implications of such a change are far-reaching.

One of the key questions we must ask ourselves is how AI will shape the experiences and development of these children. Will they view the world through a different lens, one shaped by technology and artificial intelligence? And what will be the impact of AI on family dynamics and relationships? How will it shape the way we interact with one another and the values we hold dear?

Moreover, as AI continues to play an increasingly vital role in our lives, we must consider the ethical implications of this technology. Privacy and autonomy are crucial components of a free and democratic society, and we must be vigilant in our efforts to protect them. At the same time, we must also recognize the potential of AI to solve global problems and create a better future.

I hope that this book will inspire the next generation to think deeply about the role of AI in our lives and to use their creativity and innovation to shape a fairer and more sustainable world. It is the collective actions of every one of us that will decide the future of AI and the impact it has on our society. The responsibility rests with us to ensure that it is a future that is just and compassionate.

*The potential for kids born under
AI control to shape the future*

Now we will reflect on the unique position of kids born under AI control and the potential they hold to shape the future.

From birth, these kids have been immersed in a world where technology and AI play a leading role. They have grown up with access to vast amounts of information and the ability to communicate and connect with people all over the world. This presents a significant advantage when it comes to shaping the future of AI and technology.

These kids are the first generation to have a comprehensive understanding of both the potential and the limitations of AI. They can bring a fresh perspective and current ideas to the table. With their technological fluency and innovative thinking, they are well-equipped to shape the future in positive ways.

These kids have the potential to create a fairer and more sustainable world. With AI as a tool, they can work towards solving global problems, such as poverty, climate change, and disease. They can use the power of technology to create more efficient systems and processes, reducing waste and improving the quality of life for people all over the world.

However, this potential can only be realized if we provide these kids with the education, support, and opportunities they need to thrive. This means creating a culture that values creativity, innovation, and ethics. We must encourage these kids to think critically and independently, question assumptions, and challenge the status quo. Only then will they be able to fully realize their potential and shape the future in ways that help all of us.

Kids born under AI control hold a unique position in shaping the future of technology and society. With the right support and education, they have the potential to create a better world for us all. As we close this book, let us reflect on the themes and questions explored and take inspiration from the potential of these kids to shape the future for the common good.

Understanding and preparing for the impact of AI

In the rapidly strengthening technological landscape, the impact of artificial intelligence on the next generation is a topic of great concern and fascination. As we delve deeper into this new era of AI, we must take the time to understand and prepare for the changes that are to come.

As philosopher Alan Watts once said, "The only way to make sense out of change is to plunge into it, move with it, and join the dance." In the same vein, we must embrace the changing landscape of AI and learn to dance with its impact on the next generation.

At the heart of this issue lies the question of what it means to be human. As AI continues to advance and become integrated into our daily lives, inevitably, it will also shape the childhood experiences and development of the next generation. Will their relationship with AI shape these children in ways that will redefine what it means to be human?

It is our responsibility as a society to think critically about the role that AI should play in shaping the next generation. We must be mindful of the ethical and fair implications of our actions and ensure that the development of AI is guided by principles that prioritize the well-being and dignity of all.

It is also important that we recognize the potential for AI to contribute to solving global problems and creating a better future. Kids born under AI control have the unique opportunity to shape the development of AI in ways that will have a positive impact on the world. They must be equipped with the skills and knowledge to do so.

As we move deeper into the AI era, we must reflect on the themes and questions explored in this book. Let us embrace the changes to come and work together to ensure that they equipped the next generation with the tools they need to create a fairer and more sustainable world with the help of AI.

The need for continued reflection

As we delve deeper into the world of artificial intelligence, we must continue to reflect and act on the impact it will have on society, especially on the next generation of kids. The rapid pace of technological advancement presents both challenges and opportunities, and it is up to us to understand how best to harness its potential for the common good.

In considering the future of AI, we must consider the ethical implications of this powerful tool and the responsibility we ensure that someone develops responsibly it and equitably. This is not just a matter of technical ability, but of moral vision. It requires a deep understanding of the interconnectedness of all life and the importance of creating a fairer and more sustainable world for future generations.

As we prepare kids for the future workforce dominated by AI, we must equip them with the skills and qualities that will be essential in this new era. This includes fostering creativity, innovation, and critical thinking, as well as an understanding of the ethical implications of AI and the importance of contributing to the debate about its future.

At the same time, we must be mindful of the impact that AI may have on personal privacy and autonomy. It is our responsibility to ensure that kids have the knowledge and skills to navigate this rapidly changing landscape and to advocate for their rights in the face of new and emerging technologies.

The future of AI is in our hands, and the role of kids in shaping it for the common good cannot be overstated. They are the ones who will inherit the consequences of our actions, and we must prepare them for the challenges and opportunities that lie ahead.

In the end, it is not just about the technical ability of AI, but about the moral vision that underlies its development and use. Let us use this opportunity to reflect, act, and create a more fair and sustainable future for all.

ACKNOWLEDGMENTS

First, I would like to express my deep gratitude to the young minds of our future, who inspired me to draft this book and shed light on the complexities of a world under AI control. Their unwavering spirit and drive to create a better world filled me with hope and encouraged me to delve deeper into the subject.

I would also like to extend my appreciation to the experts in the field of AI, psychology, education, philosophy, and ethics, who generously shared their insights and knowledge with me. Your contributions were invaluable and enriched my understanding of the subject.

Additionally, I would like to thank my family and friends for their unwavering support and encouragement throughout the writing process. Your love and encouragement kept me motivated and gave me the strength to see this project to completion.

To all of you, I am deeply grateful for your support and for helping me bring this book to life. May it inspire future generations to shape a world that is fair, sustainable, and filled with endless possibilities.

www.ingramcontent.com/pod-product-compliance
Lightning Source LLC
Chambersburg PA
CBHW070320220526
45465CB00013B/1898